How
and be W
into your new
Country Life

10 aspects of life to get right when you escape to the country

A Pendown Pocket Book

How to Fit-In and be Welcomed
into your new Country Life
ISBN:978-1-909936-12-6

Copyright 2017 - All Rights Reserved –
Pendown Pocket Books

'Pendown Pocket Books' is a wholly owned
subsidiary of Pendown Publishing UK.
All rights belong to Pendown Publishing
Cornwall UK.

Set in Gentium Book Basic

Paperback edition Pendown Publishing
Cornwall UK 2017
Pendownpublishing.co.uk

Cover: PP Designs

Introduction:

Welcome to this guide to fitting into your new chosen environment. We all want to feel comfortable where we live, want to fit in and enjoy living amongst our new friends and neighbours – this guide will help you achieve this without putting your foot in it – and there's plenty of it in the countryside to put your foot in!

Table of Contents

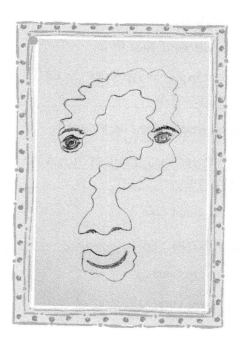

Chapter 1   Who Are You?

Everyone is a stranger

The thing about moving to the countryside is that everyone knows everyone else - maybe not by name, but certainly by sight.

So, as a newcomer you will be an object of interest. People will wonder – who you are. Now this is not affected by age, race or creed. Everyone gets the once-over until everyone else knows who the new person is.

Using the Grapevine

The best way to get over this awkward stage is make sure that the right people know who you are, and this is where you can 'leak' just the information you want to get out.

If you are lucky enough to have escaped to a village with a local shop or post office, or even, wonders upon wonders, both – then use it! Start with ordering your papers there. You will have to give your name as a start and it will be easy to say 'I've just moved in to Rose cottage' in natural conversation.

Over the next few days picking up your paper you will soon get drawn into conversation with the shop owners and can sow the seeds of what you want people to know about you, because, though not gossips in the malicious way, the local shop owners are disseminators of the village news – and you, for a day or so, are *it*.

Extending the Grapevine

Close on the heels of the Village shop, or if your village has lost it, comes the pub. Here it is not so easy to get your message across, 'who you are', that you are now a 'local' but after a visit or two the landlord may realise you are not just a passing stranger and may pass a moment of two in conversation with you. The operative plan is similar to the village shop – though you may find the dissemination of the news slower this way.

Villages without a heart

If your village has neither of these establishments then it will be a sorry excuse for a village. You will have to seek out wherever it is that the locals hang out – and get yourself over there to infiltrate the network and get yourself identified at a glance. This may have to be the pub in the next village over or you may have to look into a different kind of establishment.

But maybe with a soul

Even villages that have lost both shop and pub often still retain a church of some description, sometimes two, offering you a choice between C of E and the other one. If you move in near a big festival, Easter, Harvest, Christmas, then you may get yourself along and get known without a full commitment – like everywhere they are used to high-days and holy-days attendees. If you want to be welcomed with open arms, and are inclined, become a regular.

Note: in *most* UK villages the choice of places of worship is historically limited to variations of a Christian theme, but not everywhere.

TIP:
When you do get introduced to people make sure you hear and remember the other person's name. It will be easy for them – you are the stranger and they will learn your name easily, if they didn't already know it, and thereafter greet you by name ... so you'll need to be able to do the same.

Jean was introduced to a very nice lady who said she used to be the cleaner for the previous owners of Jean's new home. She missed hearing the lady's name, or forgot it almost straight away - as it is so easy to do in these circumstances. She says: even two years later the lady still greets her by her first name ... yet she has never felt able to re-ask the lady's name and so can't reply the same back. (Obviously the trick is to ask at the shop – they know everything!)

Chapter 2   Attending

How to get a good name in the village

Arm yourself

A lively village will have a plethora of activities going on. First arm yourself with the designated list. This may be a village diary, or news sheet, or it may be a glossy booklet, or a less than glossy leaflet. Whatever it is – it is gold-dust for showing you the muscles beneath the skin, what makes this place tick. In fact, when you are planning your escape it is always a good idea to lay hands on these items before settling on a property in the country – then you will know you are not moving to a heartless, soulless and dead village but one with some vigour.

You may have to live in the village for a whole year to understand the scope of what goes on, but even one month's offering will give you an idea.

Look out for posters too, they may be homemade or lacking in layout and design – but you can bet they are heartfelt and about things of interest to the village.

Make a sortie
Choose some general events to go along to - coffee mornings, afternoon teas, the church bazaar, the school fete, the village gala day, the football club car-boot sale

– whatever is on, go along and support it. You may only buy a cake and a cuppa, or try you hand at the tombola but it will be noticed, you will be seen as someone who supports the village. One shiny-star point to you!

Breach some defences

There are many clubs that hold an open day or evening, to encourage new people to join. Or you can just go along to a regular meeting. This is a deeper infiltration, and you must be prepared for it to be assumed that you will join, or at least be hoped for.

There are exceptions - it is always safe, for instance, for a man to go along to a WI open evening, *when* it says *'men too'*, as he's not going to be asked to join – and they always have a speaker that they think men will enjoy for these – so it is a win-win, a good talk, a cup of tea a slice of cake and a nice chat to the locals.

Show your colours

When it comes to the competitive side of village life tread carefully. Make sure you go along as a observer, in the first year at least, to the village produce show, the village horse, dog or what-have-you show. Any competitive event – observe and be seen. Next year you can have a go – but read 'Chapter 5 Joining In' before you do.

On the other hand, if there is a communal event going on where you can show your commitment to the village, then go along, these include things like village-wide litter-picks, clearing roadside verges of ragwort or helping in a community orchard or garden.

Do not neglect you first port of call either, remember the local shop is the disseminator of news, and those who regularly buy a selection of products will not only do the village good by helping to keep this tiny beating heart operating, but will engender good wishes from the proprietors as well – the few extra pence spent will be well worth it.

Win the day
By being interested, by showing your face, by supporting the local causes, without being flashy, you will win the day. Villages like to be inclusive, they like everyone to become part of the village and that is also your aim.

Chapter 3   Driving

How to fit-in behind the Wheel

Slim Down:
We are not talking of literally fitting behind the wheel here, but of the type of car you chose to drive.
There is, of course, your car you have already, but is it suitable for your transition to the countryside?

The expansive expensive saloon: Unless you are not bothered by a few (lots of) scratches down the sides of your car, then this may not be a suitable car for the countryside. If you love your car, and can afford it, then by all means keep your prestige car for your trips to the big city – but keep it off the narrow lanes.

The fat 4x4 you already drive – or envisage yourself needing in the countryside: Don't - just don't! BIG flashy 4x4s are not necessary (despite the pot-holes) and are usually too W I D E to be a comfortable drive for you (or others you meet) Yes, you will see plenty of proper country people driving them, but then they already live in the countryside and may actually need to go off-road and they won't worry about ramming the side of their vehicle into the hedge to let you get by.

If you have bought LAND with your home and need a 4x4 to lug stuff across it, then get a second-hand hard-work Land Rover type of vehicle and you'll fit right in.

The little second-hand runner: *Yes!* Yes do get a car that you can happily allow to get scratched by brambles and thorns as you squeeze in to let the fat 4x4 get past. Feel smug as you nip around the pot-holes, learn to handle meeting anything with equanimity and not a care for your paintwork; tractor, muck-spreader or mud-on-the-road will not worry you a jot.

The little second-hand runner!

Beef-up – on the unwritten rules:
There are aspects of driving that take on a whole new precedence when you move to the countryside and you would do well to make sure you are proficient and absorb these 'laws'.

Reversing:

Many lanes are one car wide, with occasional passing places (more on these later) so it is obvious that you will meet another car on one of these at sometime.

You need to be,
1, aware of where the last passing place you have passed actually was ...
2, be ready to reverse back to it, unless
a, you know the other driver is much closer to a passing place than you are, or
b, you already have someone behind you on the road, and they do not, or
c, they are useless at reversing (and demonstrate it by going up the hedge in at least two different directions) - and you want to show off your skill!

There are actual highway rules that say to give way to the person driving uphill when you can - but this does not always play out in practice, especially if it means reversing a long way uphill and round a bend! Nor does the rule that says you should never reverse more than a specific distance – if it did then some of us would still be stuck on some back lanes! The Highway Code says, no person shall drive a vehicle 'backwards on a road further than may be requisite for the safety or reasonable convenience of the occupants of the vehicle or other traffic.'

In case you missed it **REVERSING is the main driving skill** you need to be proficient in – unless you want to endure the LOOK – the one that says 'Why are you even ON a country road if you can't reverse??'

A note on meeting another car on a narrow road at night:
There you are, both with headlights blazing and you meet between two passing places. Usually the more confident driver will begin to reverse. DO NOT move towards them as they do! It doesn't help and restricts any adjustment manoeuvres they may need

to make if the road is particularly winding.

DO turn your headlights OFF. Yes OFF. You will retain your side lights – no-one will think you have disappeared. You will still be able to see as the reversing driver will have his lights on AND they will be able to see behind them much better by their reversing light without being blinded by your headlights.

This way you will both be on your way much faster... and don't forget the double flick to say 'thank you' when you get to pass! (see: the wave exercise below)

Passing places:

Hell knows no wrath like that reserved for the idiot who PARKS in a passing place. Passing places (labelled or not) are any space wide enough for two cars to pass in what is otherwise a one-car-wide road. Rule 156 of the Highway Code covers this! Only if TWO cars could pass side by side **and** leave room for a stationary car, does a dip in the hedge/wall/ditch line become a parking spot!

Blindingly obvious:
Winding roads mean very short lines of sight. Even at 30 mph, two cars seeing each other on the cusp of a blind bend would have, perhaps, ten to fifteen meters to stop themselves from colliding at a combined speed of 60 miles an hour. Even with feet fully on the brakes there is nowhere to go – the choice may be: head on collision / into the hedge/wall / down over the bank / into the ditch / into a tree trunk?

Blind corners on one-car-wide roads have to be approached as if there is a car coming towards you around that bend. Though it may not be a car, it may just be a family out for a walk with their dog, a cyclist, a horse-rider, a wild animal, like a deer or a badger, or even a cow or a pony. Around a blind bend is an invisible place – and every road user should enter it with care.

From the horse's mouth:
Talking of horses - a horse has a right to be on the road, and you have the duty to pass that horse with extreme care - for the safety of horse and rider - and your door-panels! On wide roads you will pass safely, as wide as you can and as gently and quietly as you can - of course.
However, on the narrow lanes it is also a matter of patience.
If the horse is coming towards you, pull in and let the rider steer their horse past you. You will receive a cheery wave for this.
If you are behind the horse - hold back! Trickle along at the pace of the horse - the rider should be aware you are there and will find the first safe place to pull in that they can. However, this may take patience as passing places can be few and far between. Never crowd the horse and

rider - it will not help speed things up at all. When they do find a place to pull in, or the road becomes wide enough, pass quietly, slowly and as far away from the beast as possible.

Toot-Toot:
If you think you need to break the peace of the countryside with tooting before every blind bend - you are going **too fast**. Enough said.

Warning lights:
Some seem to think that driving at night means that those blind corners can be 'seen' around as they would see the lights from another car coming towards them. Another car – yes, but not a group of teenagers walking back from their friend's, nor the man walking his dog before bedtime, or a wild or domesticated animal. Blind bends are blind whatever time of the day or night.

Exercise your way to fit-in behind the wheel

The 'Wave' exercise

Someone reversed for you to pass in a narrow lane - wave!

Someone waited in a wide bit for you to come through - wave!

Someone slowed down as they passed you while you were walking – wave!

Someone pulled in tighter to the hedge to let you through easier (on a tight two-car-wide road) - wave!

On the other hand, if you do this for anyone else and they wave thanks to you; you will also give them a wave of acknowledgement of their thanks to you! Got that?

You, of course, will perfect your own version; the range is wide - from a thumbs up or a raised forefinger (like a blessing) through a quick palm to screen to an almost full- blown salute!

The night-time version of this wave is a very quick flick of the headlights.
Scorn falls upon those who do not exercise this simple courtesy!

The Parish Smile and Wave – *further exercises to help you fit-in*

Not just for the local vicar – smile and wave at anyone you pass in the whole of your village (or even Parish) and you will get to be known as the friendly new person (rather than the stuck-up / grumpy new person). It doesn't matter if you are driving or walking – anyone passing should be given a demonstration of this 'smile and wave' exercise.

Exercising your intention:

Talking about signalling to others with a wave and a smile leads to the conventional signals drivers give. Generally country people still signal their intent to turn, at junctions and on roundabouts. Do not be surprised if your lack of indication is frowned upon – if not actually hooted at.

Working-out - on the roads
Farm vehicles are not there to clog up the roads and cause trouble. They are only out on the country roads because they need to get to their place of work. Yes, they can spread mud (which will be scraped up later) Yes they are BIG. Yes, they are slow (You really do not want to meet one going fast along these country lanes) BUT they belong in the countryside – it is the farmer and the farm that makes so much of our countryside as we expect it to be.

Chapter 4   Walking

Nice and slowly does it

Walking is a pleasant pastime in the countryside and a great way to help yourself fit in. You will both get to know your way around and get to know people.

Wherever you walk in the countryside – remember to **Follow the Country Code**: Here is a summary from the Government website: (full details in the appendix)

Respect other people:

- consider the local community and other people enjoying the outdoors

- leave gates and property as you find them and follow paths unless wider access is available

Protect the natural environment:

- leave no trace of your visit and take your litter home

- keep dogs under effective control

Enjoy the outdoors:

- plan ahead and be prepared
- follow advice and local signs

Let's look at some different kinds of walk you might try:

The Constitutional Walk:

Every day at a certain time (after lunch, after supper, after work) you take a walk. This may be the same route day after day – or a variation that still takes you in a circle back to your home.

On this kind of walk you will pass the same places frequently – and see people - particularly in the warmer months. You can cheerfully say 'Good Afternoon' and expect to receive the same back. When they've got used to you (and checked you out with the village shop / pub/

whatever) they may graduate to a longer sentence ... or you may ... 'What a wonderful display of Dahlias – are you entering the village show?' kind of thing should break the ice.

The Explorative walk:
Armed with a large map of the parish you may walk different areas, particularly trying to link up some of the marked footpaths. Again, you will meet and pass some places frequently on your outward or homeward bound forays – employ the same tactics as above to engage the locals in conversation.

The Dog-Walking walk:
This is the easiest type of walker to be if your aim is to meet people – but also the most fraught in other ways.

People you pass will often open the conversation with your dog first – before glancing up to look at the owner. They know you are new – they know they don't know you – yet, but the dog doesn't and will open channels for conversations to flow.

On the other hand – if your dog is aggressive – un-controlled – not managed properly – deposits excrement that you do not pick up and dispose of correctly – then both you and your dog could be worse off than if you stayed at home.

MORE on Dogs – and fitting in to your country life:

For your own safety: Don't go into a field that has cattle in it with your dog – not even if there is a footpath right-of-way. Of course, you are allowed – but the cows don't know that –and they tend to react to dogs in unusual ways, sometimes crowding them, or chasing them – which, as you may have seen from reports, has occasionally resulted in death – of the owner of the dog.

In any field that contains livestock even the most well-behaved dog should be on a lead. Also, be aware that dogs tend to believe where they walk is their territory (they mark it as they go) and so, should they ever escape the confines of your garden, they will most likely follow their walking routes – and if you frequently take them into a field with livestock this is where they may go. And, yes, a farmer is within their rights to shoot a dog found to be worrying sheep – and we don't mean by barking 'mint-sauce' at it.

The most contentious subject – Dog POO

Dog poo should never be flicked over the hedge into pasture fields as it can bring pathogens to the pasture that can harm livestock.

Dog poo should be picked up and bagged and TAKEN HOME or PUT IN A PROPER BIN! (not stuffed in a rabbit hole, or between rocks, or hung on a hedge or on a tree or flung into a field or a stream or hidden behind the post box ... yes – these are all real-life examples.) Apart from being just plain disgusting behaviour the bagged excrement can still be a danger to livestock and wildlife.

If you do not believe this subject is contentious – visit the Parish Council meetings.

Be the Best
The most responsible countryside walker of any type goes 'the extra mile' and carries an old carrier-bag to collect litter that disgusting people have thrown out of their cars or dropped to spoil the countryside.

TIP:
If you are new to living in the countryside you may not realise how DARK it can get once the sun goes down. If you are going out, and will be walking back late, remember to take a TORCH.

Pat and Gill had moved to a country village only that summer, both had been born and brought up in cities. One evening in early Autumn they walked to the pub – there was a folk duo playing and they stayed late. When they stepped out into the crisp night air they soon realised that it was dark outside – very dark. A moonless night meant they walked carefully along the crest of the camber in the road, glancing towards the lights from the curtained windows of the houses near the pub, trying to keep on track. Soon they had left those lights behind and as they stumbled toward the lane their cottage was down they began to walk with their arms outstretched in case they walked into something. They did, all of a sudden they stepped into the stream that ran beside the road! Feet wet, and still feeling their way, they vowed to always carry a torch when they went out in the evening!

Chapter 5   Joining-In

Deeper Infiltration
How to join-in to enhance your life and that of your new community (without causing ructions)

What are you interested in?
You will have followed the instructions in Chapter Two and 'Attended' and 'Observed' various village events and now you want to join-in.

Stage one: You have chosen the local interest groups you want to join. This is the easy part – join the group, team, project whatever you are interested in. You will be welcomed with open arms. Get to know the people (this is your main aim, after all) get to know how the group works – do not be prejudiced by your former city-life's time-scales and expectations.

Do not rush in with your own ideas of how to change how things are done – it doesn't matter if you were a managing director before you retired, or a judge or a chief constable – in the village you are still 'the newcomer'.

Observe the operation from the inside now – and if you want to influence things wait for the elections and wait to be asked to stand. Frustrating as it is – you are better to be nominated, though you should let it be known you are willing. (note: these groups always seem to be looking for treasurers with accounting abilities!)

Stage Two, once on the committee take it slow – change comes best slowly and without fuss in the countryside. Do not try to change everything all at once, or even one thing too quickly. Make sure you have seen how everything works before trying to alter it. Listen when they tell you that your idea 'has been tried before' – it probably has – but check on details and, if you can, make clear the differences and take on the burden of the exercise to see it through.

Remember it is not 'just you' the way things work are like this for everyone – it is just that they have learnt more patience – as everything does, indeed, happen slower in the countryside (It's one of the reasons you came – really)

Doing Your Own Thing - *Setting up your own interest group*
Can't find anything to interest you at all in the village events?

You can always try to set up your own interest group – be it a book group, ramblers or bird-watching. In a village you are likely to find a few others to join you.

Use those village magazines / leaflets / news-sheets you read before you moved to your countryside retreat to get the word out. Hold an open meeting at your village meeting place (Hall / Pub / Church) and off you go! Fitting in at the same time as standing out – as someone willing to add to the community! Not a bad thing.

PARISH POLITICS

Parish Council
You might decide that being elected to the Parish Council is a responsible and influential thing to do. If this is your inclination make sure you go to plenty of the council meetings first – to get the gist of the scope of items that they deal with - from planning to dog-poo!

Sometimes, if the parish council loses a member between elections, then they can co-opt. Regular attendees at meetings are sometimes asked if they would like to be a member and can be co-opted. Everyone gets to be up for election eventually.

Stage Two as above – applies in this circumstance too.

The PCC (Parochial Church Council)

If you are a regular attendee, and on the Church electoral role, you may wish to stand for the PCC. This is not so easy to get to know the ins and outs of without asking questions of those who are members already. This, of course, would signal your interest – so be ready to be asked.

Most village C of E churches are old – ancient even – and frequently listed, often at grade one, thereby requiring people skilled in making grant applications and form filling to help raise the monies required to keep them ship-shape and watertight for the future generations and the heritage of the British countryside.

If this is your skill set you will be as welcome as the people who tend to our ancient places of worship in more physical ways and raise funds by other, more traditional, means.

The running of community owned spaces:
This may be the village hall, the allotment society, a community playing field or orchard.

The 'rules' above apply. Attend open meetings, especially the AGM, and get to understand what they are about and the responsibilities that go with joining one of these groups. They are usualy, essentially, a management committee – but good people are always needed to keep these facilities going, including fund-raising and practical work.

Show your face, show your interest, and, if and when you are on the committee take it easy, do not denigrate the efforts of those who have held this torch before.

Chapter 6

Shopping & Supporting

Support your local community – how it is done!

Shop Local

We've already discussed the local shop (and Post Office – if you are lucky enough to have one). The fact is LUCKY really means that people in the village have, over the years, supported the facility enough for it to survive. However, many are on the brink of extinction at the moment as people do not realise the danger and prefer to shop all at once at the supermarket.

'You never know what you've got 'til it's gone' says the old song – but it is so true. Many villages have failed to support their local shop only to find it closed as the owners could not even make a modest living out of it. Then, realising the huge hole in the fabric of their society, the villagers have had to scrape together volunteers and money to set up their own community run version – often set up in the back room of the village hall or similar. How much better to have retained it in the first place – especially when it is relatively easy to do?

If everybody in the village made a list of everyday items that they used on a regular basis and that the shop stocks – then *always* bought those items at the local shop – it would survive. Many village shops stock at least one variety each of the basic non-food stuffs – cleaning products, stationery, cards, etc plus cans, jars, packets and bottles of foods with long dates on them. If you are lucky to have a shop that also has fresh goods (much harder for them to actually stock) then add these to your list – whatever you can – then ALWAYS buy these specific items from your local shop – THIS will help keep it open and part of the heart of a thriving village.

If you are lucky enough to still have a Post Office – use it for all your posting, and banking, needs! Most banks have an agreement with the Post Office now.

Now you have stocked up on your basics you can turn to see what else is available without leaving your Parish.

Farms, Small-holdings and Nurseries
Many farms have diversified and now sell direct from the farm. This may be vegetables and fruit – but it may also be meat and meat products. Almost no food-miles when you buy local! At the same time you get to know the producers – and these are often the real locals who have held their farms for generations. Word will get out that you are really making an effort to support the local community.

Depending on your area there may also be plant nurseries or flower producers, maybe designed to sell on to garden centres and such, but selling some direct to the local customers at local prices. Frequently this is by 'honesty boxes' or 'open at the weekend' type stalls, but still a great local resource and a good place to get to meet locals who know where to go for the best plants and flowers.

Many of these are set up by those locals running a small-holding – usually too small to be a farm, but of enough acres to produce a regular flow of goods. Newer to the scene are 'community gardens' – orchards or market-gardens with the community volunteers sharing what they need and selling on what they do not, to help support the community garden.

'Honesty Box' stalls abound in the true countryside where no-one would dream of taking goods (veg, fruit, flowers – even eggs) without leaving the requisite money – a charming addition to the local scene and a source of really fresh produce – often picked that very day.

Local Tradespeople

Whether you are looking for a builder, carpenter, fencer, roofer, plumber, electrician, painter or even kitchen and bathroom fitter - you may find that there are local businesses you can support -

often more than one, so you can still get comparative quotes and yet stay local.

Ask in the usual places - the pub, the shop or from your new country friends - for recommendations, they'll know who's reliable and good value.

And while we're talking of businesses - don't forget there's mobile hairdressers, podiatrists and even pet-groomers.

SUPPORTING

All communities seem to run fund-raising events. In a village, however, you may be surprised at the wide range of causes and charities supported.

There will be the parochial – the Village Hall, the Church / Chapel / the football club / the cricket club etc. etc.

Then there will be many organised by individuals or other groups but raising funds for almost any charity or cause you can think of – from refugees and rescue organisations to assistance dogs or a school in India.

Whatever it is – do go along and support it! ...

But if you can't ...
If you really do not want to spend half an afternoon to win a packet of bath cubes on the tombola and buy a sponge cake (or are really unable to because you are out) then find out who the organiser is and drop an envelope in their door with a donation and a note apologising for missing the event. This is then a win-win for your standing in the community, for the community and for the charity.

If your funds are limited maybe you can support in other ways – with your time (to help set up / clear / do the teas / run stalls / arrange publicity - for example) and you will be welcomed with open arms. Always a good move if you want to fit into your village - but be aware that it will usually be an annual event!

Chapter 7

Getting on with the Neighbours

Don't put your foot in it

Relatives
This can not be said often enough – or in big enough letters
Don't criticise other people in the village / parish
to anyone apart from your own family.

You really (REALLY) will not be able to tell who is related to whom. The professor may be the sister of the odd-job gardener! The mechanic may be first cousin to the bank manager! Or, if not directly related then their cousin is married to that person, or they are a second cousin of the wife of the person you are talking to!

If you feel you must vent your ire about a person (to your family) – make sure you are within your own walls – the countryside has ears – as in voices travel a long way in these peaceful places, without the background white-noise of traffic.

City Ex-pats

It might be tempting to slot into a group of other exiles from the city – people 'like you' with the same backgrounds or occupations – but resist! Joining in with these isolationists (who do little for their community) will not endear you to the locals or help you integrate. Save their friendship, if you must be friends with them (they will make overtures it is certain), for the occasional dinner party. These people will only serve to deepen mistrust and reinforce any doubts while regaling you with stories of how they 'tried to change things' when they came – but were rebuffed. Or you may even become an evangelist on behalf of

Fitting-In better to the rural community – but, once their views are entrenched, you will have difficulty making decent headway.

Finding your niche

Make friends amongst those who you meet at the groups and organisations you have decided to join.

Look at traditional groups as well as the more modern; Choirs, Bell-Ringing, Ramblers, WI (open to all women over 18), Darts, Snooker, Football, Cricket, Morris-dancing as well as the Tai-Chi, Pilates, slimming groups, belly-dancing and Yoga.

If you have young children then a local playgroup or *primary school will afford you with lots of new contacts.

*If your village has a primary school then you are indeed blessed – support it in as many ways as you can – regardless of whether you have children – for a village with a primary school is more likely to be one with a true cross generational profile and be more vibrant as a result.

Re-read Chapter 4 on Walking, and see Chapter 9 on Gardening, for more ideas of how to find your new group of friends.

"We don't have any neighbours"

WHO are your Neighbours?

Not who you think

We talk of getting on with your neighbours – and in a town of city it is self-evident who your neighbours are. They live next door, or opposite, at least in your street. In the countryside you may have neighbours like these but you will, most likely, also be neighbours with the local farmer – or farmers, depending on how the field ownership/ rental works where you have chosen to live.

The land they farm is the same to them, as both your workplace AND your own back garden, are to you.

Think about that for a moment. How would you feel if someone invaded your workplace or your back garden?

There will be footpaths across some land – stay on them. Use them considerately leaving nothing behind you except your footprints (as they say) leave no litter, not even biodegradable litter (as this may cause problems to animals or contamination that you may not know about or understand) and do no damage to crops. (By the way – grass is a crop in the countryside – if not actually being grazed it is probably being grown for silage or hay – trampled flat it is difficult to harvest and may be ruined)

The much flaunted 'right to roam'

Despite what the newspapers may lead us to believe, the 'right to roam' does NOT give you the right to wander all over farmland (no more than it gives anyone the right to wander all over your back garden) The Right to Roam is restricted to certain areas, notably unfenced moorlands, uplands and the dales. Be sure of your rights before exercising them.

A brief resume of 'The Right to Roam' is in the Appendix with links listed to the Government websites. It is worth reading.

In reality, many farmers don't mind letting their friends and neighbours walk across their fields - if there are no safety or economic reasons for this not to be permitted.

This little guide is all about how to become that friend and neighbour.

Chapter 8

The 'Peace' of the Countryside

Not as much Aural as Visual

Yes, the countryside is always peaceful - BUT at times it doesn't sound peaceful.

Peaceful is a strange concept. It can refer to a quietness of sound, but that is not the only meaning. Gazing upon a green and pleasant view, still and unchanging, is peaceful. This visual peacefulness is a balm to the soul – even the colour is supposed to calm our brainwaves. This you can expect, however, **aural** peace is not guaranteed in the countryside!

Let's start early, say 4 am in the Summer when the dawn chorus, from plenty of little birds, can be very noisy indeed! Add in a local cockerel (an accepted part of the countryside – without which there would be no baby chicks!) and your day is off to a noisy start.

As this is Summer you will notice the tractors zipping around to get to the fields to cut, turn or bale hay, haylage or silage – or later to get the grain harvest in, trundling trailers-full back to the farm filled with grain spewed out from the combine harvester.

Some evenings, if rain is due, they will work with bright spotlights right into the night, to beat the weather. None of this is peaceful – but it IS the countryside at work, keeping it as it should be.

On the Sunday, if you are lucky to live in a village with a tower and ringers, the church bells will ring out, as they will on their rehearsal night. Quintessentially English, the sound of ringing the changes is woven into the fabric of village life.

Come evening you'll likely hear foxes bark, the keening of the buzzard, pheasants kirr-upping if your area has a shooting estate nearby (which raises and releases far more birds than are ever shot) crows and rooks cawing as they return to roost.

Then in Autumn, flailing the hedges to cut them back can sound positively industrial.

In Spring, add the eerie scream of the vixen on heat, even frogs can be really noisy in a quiet night! And the tractors are out again, ploughing and planting.

But in between – there is aural peace too – a quiet filled with small noises like bees buzzing, small birds chattering and the sound of water in a small stream.

What has all this to do with 'fitting-in'?
Well, not complaining about the usual sounds of the countryside will help. It is just annoying to hear people state that they came to the countryside for peace and then go on to complain about cows mooing, tractors working or church bells ringing.

The usual response of the locals would be a muttered 'go back to where you came from then!'

It is peaceful – but it is also a living place and needs to move, work and sing – and these things make sound.

Chapter 9
Gardening, Livestock and Wildlife

It's the Good Life

There is something quintessentially British about a garden ... and in the countryside maybe even more than everywhere else.

The Front Garden

The 'cottage garden' with its banks of mixed border plants is both a cliché and a wonder to behold, but any attractive planting is to be admired. It speaks of caring for the environment, sharing your visual creation with all who pass.

And that's where the front garden comes into this guide. Work in your front garden on your flower-beds and borders and you will attract the attention of those who are out walking.

A garden, rather like a dog, facilitates conversation – maybe you initiate the 'Good afternoon' or maybe they will - and you are off – making new acquaintances who may become friends, whether they are locals or other newcomers (following this guide).

The Back Garden

Traditionally the back garden is the preserve of the back lawn (for lounging on), the barbecue, the games of footy with the kids ... **and the fruit and vegetable garden.**

It may be hidden away from casual passers-by but it can still be a source of 'Joining-in'. If you grow your own you are bound to find categories in your local produce show that you can enter. There will often be a novice category as well as the oddities, like longest runner bean, heaviest marrow or tallest sunflower.

As with almost everything suggested in this guide – take it slow – visit your first produce show without entering, this way you will get to understand the arcane expectations behind the wordings. (for instance a 'bunch of herbs' may be judged firstly by the number of types of herbs included – before looking at their quality – whereas '3 beetroot' should be matched as a set to all look exactly the same and all be in prime condition - with tops).

Joining-In will then introduce you to a different set of people in the village and, as long as you don't get hung-up on winning, provide an extra dimension to your new life.

Many of these produce shows (which can be advertised under various names) also include cookery, art, photography and craft sections – so they are always worth looking at if your area holds one.

LIVESTOCK

Often the reason for moving to the countryside is to have 'a bit of land' and to keep your own livestock.

It may have looked fun on 'The Good Life' but keeping livestock has its responsibilities - and some of those are to your neighbours - residents and farmers both.

Chickens:
One of the easiest types of livestock to keep, chickens provide you with wholesome eggs on a regular basis and need little equipment to get started.

Unless you need to rear your own chicks (for instance if you were keeping chickens for meat rather than eggs) you will NOT need a cockerel. A cockerel, whilst more common in the countryside, is **only expected where his services are needed**. Otherwise it is eating the grain you provide and waking you AND your neighbours up at four in the morning. Choose wisely and consider your neighbours.

You will need to feed your chickens grain and layers pellets, but chickens also eat grass. For you to have those lovely healthful eggs your fowl will need access to plenty of grassy space. Too little area and they will turn it to mud. They will also need fresh water and shell and grit on a regular basis. You also need to have a snug, clean place for them to lay their eggs and a safe house to be shut in at night. Don't forget: You are responsible for making sure all your livestock are kept safe - see section on Wildlife.

How can this help you integrate? A few lovely eggs are always a welcome gift to a neighbour – or you could try an 'honesty box' stall of your own - don't under-sell the locals though. [*note – there are rules for this - you have to be careful how you describe your eggs - making sure you do not use 'industry standard' terms - your eggs must be clean (but not washed) and it is a good idea to have the date of production (or a best before date) on them. If using old boxes then previous details should be obscured - see notes in the Appendix.]

Ducks:

Are a delight, though messy creatures. They do not need a full pond, but do need something deep enough to duck their heads under and splash around in. As with chickens they will need feeding, proprietary duck-food pellets or if you cannot get this, pig-meal made up as a wet mash works well.

They will also need the safe house and nesting places (though they will drop eggs anywhere) and to be shut in at night.

Geese:

Are great guard 'dogs' but they are also quite noisy creatures. A few of their super eggs each year to the neighbours may make up for the honking, and at least they do not start at ridiculously early times in the day. Geese, like ducks need to be able to dip their head in water, at least, but will make do with a big bucket-full quite happily. They graze grass most of the time, leaving 'goose-squats' in their wake, with a soaked-grain meal to bring them into their safe house at night.

Goats or Sheep:

Even if it is 'just as a pet' there are rules for keeping goats and sheep (real RULES) which you would need to be aware of (see links in Appendix) As well as tasks that need doing regularly - like hoof trimming, worming, shearing (sheep) and many more.

Other than this you will know that they will require you to have good fencing – after all, you do not want to upset your new neighbours by your animals destroying their gardens – this will not help you fit in at all.

Pigs:

In fairly recent years it has become fashionable to keep pigs –notably of the 'cute' varieties as pets. Whatever type of pig – there are rules about keeping pigs – which must be abided by. They are there to protect the whole pig population and this means that if you ignore the rules and infection passed to the pigs kept by your neighbouring pig farmer you would be in trouble – both with DEFRA and with your neighbours.

And the rest ...

Alpacas, Llamas, Ostriches, Deer, Donkeys - etc. etc ...

Almost all livestock has some rules attached to their keeping.

Be aware, take care and follow the rules as they can have far reaching effects, for you and neighbouring farmers, if breached.

Horses and Ponies:

Not what country folk think of as 'Livestock' - but certainly what that 'bit of land' is often wanted for when escaping to the country.

It might seem obvious - but horses need more than just a field - to start with - a horse needs an equine companion - so now you have two - or a horse and a pony.

Then it is vital to provide horses with protection from poor weather conditions and from strong sunlight, so you'll need a shelter for both summer and winter use. Whichever type of shelter you choose, open or enclosed, it must protect from prevailing winds and be situated in a well-drained part of the field. Shelters should be well made, with no projections that could cause injury, and fastened into the ground to prevent them moving, being blown over in strong winds. or being pushed by horses.

If the shelter is enclosed it must be large enough for the number of horses in the field, preferably with a fenced area of hard standing.

The field should be visited at least twice per day. This is important - to check the horse and inspect the field.

It is also essential to manage the pasture properly.

At least once a week, droppings should be removed from the field and shelters.

Make sure you are able to rest some of the land, to enable it to recover and grow new grass, by either dividing the field or using strip-grazing.

Fresh, clean water must be available at all times, which means that water troughs must be kept full of fresh water, and free from ice in cold weather.

Daily inspection of feet, including being picked out is essential. Every eight weeks a professional inspection should be carried out by a farrier.

When you are thinking about your time, don't forget the grooming, the rugging (which, if used, needs checking on every day), the process of feeding and watering and changing the bedding.

Then you need to think about security for your horses. They all should be microchipped, and all gates should be padlocked safely.

And all this - without even going into the ongoing costs of feed, bedding, veterinary bills, rugs, tack and grooming products etc. etc.

WILDLIFE

Some wildlife you may have to modify your views on when you live in the countryside.

You can still like to see them – but maybe you need to know what the realities are before you share your views about them with your new country neighbours.

Foxes:
Beautiful when glimpsed sunning themselves in the meadow – hateful when they break into the hen-house and slaughter all your lovely hens - or come in the middle of the morning – and kill as many as they can catch – leaving your back garden strewn with bloody feathers, carcasses and damaged, traumatised birds that will probably die from the shock.

Country people do not hate the fox – they know they have their place in the environment – they also know they need to be kept to reasonable numbers so that they do not need to venture into human environs to find food.

Badgers:
You will quickly learn that you cannot fence to keep out a badger. The TB discussion aside (and most country people know what they think) the explosion in badger numbers has meant that badgers, too, are coming into closer proximity to human habitats to feed; breaking into poly-tunnels, upturning glass cloches (to eat the strawberries), destroying vegetable gardens, and yes, breaking into hen / duck houses too, wreaking havoc and causing deaths.

Not only do they kill domestic poultry - the rise in badger numbers maybe the cause of the demise of **the country hedgehog.** Where, in towns and cities, it may be roads and unlinked gardens that are the problem - in the countryside the problem seems to be the rise in their main predator - the badger.

Deer:
Deer numbers have also increased vastly and they will devastate a garden overnight, again targeting the contents of poly tunnels, rose beds, vegetable gardens. Again, as they can spring over quite high fences, it is difficult to fence them out.

Pigeons:
Net your brassicas, and many other crops that the pigeons like when their leaves are tender. In some areas pigeons are a real problem to both farmer and gardener, costing agriculture millions in damaged crops

Rabbits:
The rabbit population seems to wax and wane – but at its height it causes a food (financial) loss of £100 million a year to farmers. Similar losses may occur in your

own patch, though fencing for these pests is slightly easier for you than for a farmer – just don't forget they can dig under. Ideally fences should be of 2.5cm (1-1¼in) wire mesh and 120-140cm (48-54in) in height. The bottom 30cm (1ft) should be buried below ground level, with the lower 15cm (6in) bent outwards to stop rabbits tunnelling underneath. Gates and other entrances must also be rabbit-proof and kept closed when not in use.

Squirrels and Magpies:
These two creatures have been put together for the simple reason that too many of these means fewer small birds – both will prey upon the eggs and the chicks and the fledglings of small birds.

What has this got to do with fitting-in?
Well, knowing a few, less publicised, facts about these creatures may mean you do not 'put your foot in it' by talking like a townie about wildlife in the countryside.

Chapter 10

Airing Your Views
Or perhaps not ...

Like any good dinner party AVOID Politics, Religion, the local 'Hot-potato' and a few sundry other things of note.
We all get comfortable with our own group of cronies – those people who 'share our views' - which only serves to reinforce our own prejudices.

Politics

The countryside is conservative (please note – the is with a little 'c') it does not mean that all the people in the countryside vote Conservative
Country people may vote more for the Person than the Party. Where the party has carefully chosen a genuinely good and hard working person with a real local connection – they will have a far

greater chance of winning in a country area than a similar candidate from outside the area – enough to swing the change from one to the other top contenders for that particular seat.

'Belonging' means a lot more out in the country areas as they have a strong sense of belonging.

So, do not assume you know anything about your new neighbours' political leanings – until they stand before you with a rosette on, at least.

The local 'Hot-potato'.

This will be whatever the locals have a bee-in-their-bonnet about at the time. These things come up from time to time, be it a planning application, a local scandal or damage in the allotments – do not pontificate unless you are involved. There is frequently such a long back history to these things that it is best to listen and let them sort out the pros and cons ... until the day that you are one of the people who can remember when 'an identical proposal was turned down unanimously twenty-five years ago' ... and on what grounds!

Some things are different ...
Council houses in the countryside are far more likely to be filled with the youngsters of the locals (who can't afford to buy the home you just bought) don't denigrate them – you have no idea who is related to whom – remember.

Incomers can have a poor reputation for good reasons – if they don't integrate, if they don't add to the community, if they want things done the way they are in the city. On top of which they drive up house prices so the locals can't afford to live where they grew up.

Second-Home owners.
If you have just bought your second-home in a lovely country village - you

need to work extra hard to help make that village work. Otherwise, you have effectively damaged the very fabric of the type of place you were looking for – you have created a small hole for most of the year.

The residents will know this – better say it is going to be your home, as soon as you can unshackle yourself from the city (at least that suggests you are worth getting to know).

Conclusion:

Try to follow these guidelines and you should slip into country life as easy as sliding in a cow-pat.

If you live life like a local - after twenty years or so – the real locals may forget that you do not have the requisite 'three generations in the churchyard' and consider you a local too.

A *final Anecdote:*
Bill moved to the village and got to know people, and joined in, after fifteen years he was almost indistinguishable from a local. When he retired he took up tracing his family tree. Though not from that area he discovered his great, great-granddad had been born less than half a mile away – and he now proudly claims the title of local!

APPENDIX

That useful information and those links we told you about ...

(weblinks correct when going to press)

The Right to Roam information
courtesy HMG website

https://www.gov.uk/right-of-way-open-access-land/

Your right to roam

You can access some land across England without having to use paths - this land is known as 'open access land' or 'access land'.

Access land includes mountains, moors, heaths and downs that are privately owned. It also includes common land registered with the local council and some land around the English Coastal Path.

Your right to access this land is called the 'right to roam', or 'freedom to roam'.

What you can and can't do

You can use access land for walking, running, watching wildlife and climbing.

There are certain **activities you can't** usually do on open access land, including:

- horse-riding
- cycling
- camping
- taking animals other than dogs on to the land
- driving a vehicle (except mobility scooters and powered wheelchairs)
- water sports

But **you can** use access land for horse-riding and cycling **if**:

- the landowner allows it
- public bridleways or byways cross the land – horse riders and cyclists can ride along these
- there are local traditions, or rights, of access

Dogs on open access land

You must keep your dog on a lead no more than 2 metres long on open access land:

- between 1 March and 31 July - to protect ground-nesting birds
- at all times around livestock

On land next to the England Coast Path you must keep your dog under close control.

There may be other local or seasonal restrictions. These don't apply to public rights of way or assistance dogs.

Excepted land

On access land some areas remain private ('excepted land'). You don't have the right to access these areas, even if they appear on a map of open access land.

Excepted land includes:

- houses, buildings and the land they're on (eg courtyards)
- land used to grow crops
- building sites and land that's being developed
- parks and gardens
- golf courses and racecourses
- railways and tramways
- working quarries

Use public rights of way to cross excepted land.

For full information go to:
https://www.gov.uk/right-of-way-open-access-land

THE COUNTRY CODE

(England / Wales / Scotland)
Country Code – England
https://www.gov.uk/government/public ations/the-countryside-code/the-countryside-code

Respect other people:

- consider the local community and other people enjoying the outdoors

- leave gates and property as you find them and follow paths unless wider access is available

Protect the natural environment:

- leave no trace of your visit and take your litter home

- keep dogs under effective control

Enjoy the outdoors:

- plan ahead and be prepared

- follow advice and local signs

Country Code – Wales

http://www.countrysidecodewales.or g.uk/

The Welsh countryside is beautiful, to say the least. The stunning landscapes are quite mesmerising with the beautiful valleys and mountains adding to the overall aesthetic appeal. There is a lot that is to be done in order to maintain the visual appeal of this place and as visitors or citizens, there are a few things that you can do to contribute as well. Whether you are visiting the Welsh countryside for a holiday or if you are living and working here, there is a set code that you need to follow.

So, what are the things that you are supposed to always bear in mind when living or holidaying in the Welsh countryside?

Respect people who reside in the countryside:

It is important to understand that no job is big or small. The people who reside in the countryside are responsible in some way or the other for making your visit to their place memorable. Respect them and the work they do for tourists like you.

Prevent damage to crops:

There are always pathways created for you to move around. Avoid walking on the crops and damaging them when you have a clear pathway across the farmland. Also, avoid fields where you see animals. You may cause them trouble and may also hurt yourself in return.

Understand your limits:

Most land that you see on the countryside is usually owned by agricultural farmers and landlords. It is upon their discretion to allow you or not to spend time on their land. Always check for permission before entering any property.

Educate your kids:

When you are travelling with children, it is important you give them some basic information on how they need to behave in the countryside. Littering is often punishable. You should always carry your litter back with you. Plastic and tin cans can be extremely dangerous for the grazing animals. A bigger concern for many is the children playing with animals. This may cause the farmers a lot of trouble.

Country Code – Scotland

The Scottish Outdoor Access Code

In Scotland, where there is a more general right of access, Scottish Natural heritage developed **The Scottish Outdoor Access Code:**

- · Take responsibility for your own actions

- Respect people's privacy and peace of mind

- Help farmers, landowners and others to work safely and effectively

- Care for the environment

- Keep your dog under proper control

- Take extra care if you are organising a group, an event or running a business

With wider access comes more definition, so to fully understand your rights, limits and responsibilities in Scotland – download a free ebook or pdf explaining it all from this website *http://www.outdooraccess-scotland.com/#*

DEFRA Rules for keeping livestock
Department for Environment, Food & Rural Affairs

You don't have to own animals to be a keeper. You're a sheep, goat, pig or deer keeper if you have responsibility for the day-to-day care and control of these animals. This includes a single animal kept temporarily or as a pet.

Start here for guidance as to your responsibilities as a keeper

https://www.gov.uk/government/collect ions/guidance-for-keepers-of-sheep-goats-and-pigs

WILDLIFE and COUNTRYSIDE ACT 1981 - is wide ranging and complicated. This site has a useful brief overview of part 1 (wildlife)
http://naturenet.net/law/wcagen.html

Poultry links

For lots of good information on all types of poultry this magazine website is very useful.
https://poultrykeeper.com/

And this one has a handy flow chart to guide you through the egg selling rules

http://www.ruleworks.co.uk/poultry/selling-eggs.htm

DEFRA also have their pages - but these concern large producers more than the small ones. This one with the AHVLA *(Animal Health and Veterinary Laboratories Agency)* is useful in that it references many relevant DEFRA pages.

http://ahvla.defra.gov.uk/documents/surveillance/diseases/backyard-poultry-guidance.pdf

About the author

The compiler of this guide grew up in one village, lived in the city and then moved to another village. Anecdotes and other ideas for inclusion in future editions are welcome please email
info @ pendownpublishing.co.uk

Other guides from Pendown Pocket Books

In development

Winning the Menopause War

Looking after your skin
- the natural way

Quick Weights for Weight-loss

Did you enjoy this book?

We want to thank you for purchasing and reading this book.

May we ask you a quick favour?

If you enjoyed this book we would really appreciate it if you could leave us a positive review on Amazon.

We love getting feedback from our customers and reviews on Amazon really do make a difference. We read all our reviews and would really appreciate your thoughts.

Thanks so much.
Pendown Pocket Books

For Your Own Notes: